MW01096936

Dust Shaker

Poems and Prayers for
Lectionary Year B

Thom M. Shuman

Copyright © 2014 Thom M. Shuman

All rights reserved.

ISBN: 150038660X
ISBN-13: 978-1500386603

DEDICATION

When I was a child,
not quite able to understand
what was going on
or what the preacher was saying,
I would turn to the hymnbook
and read the hymns.

From that time until now,
the music of the church –
the tunes, the words,
the psalms, the anthems, the carols –
have been an integral part
of my faith.

For the last few years,
I have been blessed
to share in worship and ministry
with Michael Fuchs,
not only a gifted musician,
but a person of great faith.

Thanks for the joy and privilege
of working with you, Mike!

Contents

ACKNOWLEDGMENTS

In addition to writing liturgies for each Sunday in the lectionary year, I have tried to write what I used to call the 'Back of the Bulletin' piece. Sometimes prayers, more often poetic, they were whispers which came to me in the middle of the night, or in the shower, or in those moments of procrastination from sermon preparation, nudges (if you will) by that muse we know as the Holy Spirit. More and more I imagine the Trinity as a three-piece group – God on the drums, the Spirit playing the upright bass, and Jesus at the piano – sometimes playing a little blues, a lot of jazz, a dash of r & b, and always, always improvising as they accompany our lives. I hope you hear them playing as you read these writings from several cycles of Year B.

especially

when we see you
not only in the twinkle
of a woman's eye
as she lets her grandchildren
lick the icing bowl,
but especially in
a homeless mother
looking at hope's
empty shelves;

when we hear you
not only in the carols
of the children
at evensong,
but especially
in the silent sobs
of the father who
has lost his job;

when we feel you
not just in the embrace
of loved ones
at the airport,
but especially
in the palsied,
paper-thin-skinned hands
of the lonely widower;

when we know you
not just in the assertive platitudes
of those who have never held a doubt,
but especially
in the shattered heart
of the teenager
whose faith has slipped
through her fingers:
then
we will know
you have come
just as you
promise.

First Sunday of Advent

kingdom, come

each morning,
goodness glides across the sky,
warming life's winter,
so that trustworthiness
can blossom in each
heart;

in the ancient cathedral,
righteousness and peace
stand before the congregation,
speaking their vows
and exchanging rings,
as God invites,
'you may now
kiss one another';

across the street,
Chesed and 'Emet
have gone into business together,
dressing the windows
and stocking the shelves
for their Advent sale;

and with grace and glory,
the baptizer has cleansed
the River 'avon
of all the impurities dumped
with reckless impunity by sin,
patiently waiting
for the kids to show up
to go for a dip;

selah

Second Sunday of Advent

come, anointing oil

when we would place
a foreclosed sign
on the ash-strewn lawn
of disappointed dreams,
you come,
hanging a wreath
strung together
from hope and peace
with a great, glittery
bow of grace;

when we would hand
the outcasts
the cast-offs from
our closets,
you come,
wrapping them in
your handknitted shawl
(from the finest Lambs' wool)
of embracing joy;

when we would
lash the broken
to that never-ending round
of paperwork, regulations
and platitudes,
you come,
slipping the shackles off,
laughing together
as you race to frolic
in the Spirit's sprinklers.

come, grace's fragrance;
come, love's lotion;
come, compassion's comfort;

come, and anoint us with
you!

Third Sunday of Advent

i don't have time

bone-weary from errands

i don't have time to listen
  to my children singing in the tub,
  to my spouse quietly fixing dinner,
  to the angel whispering in my ear;

exhausted from the mall expeditions

i don't have time to wait
  to find hope stuffed in my mailbox,
  to see you walking with me in the snow,
    for you to fill my emptiness;

spending the whole weekend decorating

i don't have time
  to greet a neighbor with a smile
    and not a mumble,
  to scrape the ice off my heart
    so you won't slip and fall,
  to be rocked gently
    in the cradle of your love.

      but
here i am,
  Lord,

  hoping you have
      time

for me.

Fourth Sunday of Advent

the bothy

every room will be blazing with
light,
so i will have no trouble
finding the place
when i arrive, or so i
imagine:

the table covered in fine
lace,
heirloom china
and mirrored silver at each
place
with the feast's aroma
drifting in from the kitchen;

my feather bed will manger
my weary body while
silk sheets swaddle me to sleep
after a relaxing soak
in the jet-streamed tub.

but

what if it is
just a box built out of
river rocks,
the door wind-weathered
and water-buckled,
refusing to stay shut
as if expecting more folks;
a rough-hewn shelf
in one of the corners
holds a clay pitcher brimmed
with cool clear water,
a hand-drawn map to the spring
next to it;
wood has been laid
in the fireplace,
ready to be brought to
life;

6

a stone bed is all that keeps
one's body from the ground,
just wide and long enough
for a rough blanket,
a candle and matches
where the pillow would be;
and there's a shovel
by the door for taking care
of the necessaries;

it seemed perfect for
you
when you arrived,

didn't it?

Christmas Eve

so we

you came,
    not for the carols
        sung by candlelight
     but so we
   could hear the
   broken lullabies
    of parents who
    work a double shift
       while their children
       are asleep;

you came
    not for homilies
    and meditations (however
         perfectly polished)
     but so we
  might stammer
     the good news;
    that our lives of service
        and humility
   speak louder
   than any words;

you came
    not so we
         would
    isolate ourselves
    with parties and
       pageants,
   but so we
 might enact
       the mystery
     of your coming,
  with deeds of
       justice and
    peace.

Christmas Day

simeon's song

when she grew old enough
to think she was a child again,
i held my mother's hands
on our nighttime search
for her lost doll;

when he withered
from the injustices
of a society
which told him
that if he only worked harder
he wouldn't be so poor,
i urged my friend
to be a light
to their shadowed beliefs;

when she came home
weeping
from the remarks
of her classmates
because she was 'too smart'
for their crowd,
i comforted my sister
as she wept;

and now,
i cradle in my arms
the Sympathy of the sorrowing,
the Good Samaritan of the broken,
the Finder of the lost,
the Keeper of the promises,
the Redeemer of the outcasts . . .

and i can go,
at peace,
into your Heart.

First Sunday after Christmas

9

when?

not when
      the stars
    were perfectly
     aligned;

not when
    the scientists
and
    the theologians
were on the
     same page;

not when
    the politicians
      finally reached
           across
the polarization
to agree on a course
     of action;

not when
    we had
      finally
caught on,
    listened,
      acted upon
all you had taught us
over all the centuries;

    but

when
your heart
was so stuffed
with grief
it was ready to burst,

then
     you came

fully.

Holy Name

one new thing

when i woke this
                morning,
        i would have slipped
        into that crisp, starched
                buttoned-down-collar
                        dress shirt
                i gifted to myself

                        but

        you hand me that robe
                        you wore when
                you feed the 5000
                        on the hillside,

        you slip my feet
                        into those sandals
                worn smooth by
                        your journeys
                        up and down
                        the streets of the
                                kingdom,

        around my waist
                        you wrap that towel
                still showing the heels
                        of the feet of your
                                friends
                        washed in your tears
                        on that night so long
                                        ago;

        looking at me
                from head to foot,
                        you nod,
                        whispering,

                'now

        you're ready for the new
                        year.'

New Year's Day

sirach

she has lost
                    track
of all the generations
who sat on the floor
          watching her move
          the figures around
                    the flannel board
          telling them the stories
          she knows by heart,
but we remember
                    every word,
          her voice filled with love,
          her eyes sparkling with joy,
          her tender touch of hope.

she is always at the door,
          opening it wide and
                    giving us a hug,
          steering us toward the
                              kitchen table
where the cold milk
and still warm cookies wait,
                    and as we settle into
                    the feast, she asks,
'so, tell me, how was today?'

at night, she
          plugs in the light,
tucks us safe under
          the covers,
kisses us good night,
                    and
          settles herself
          in the rocker
over in the corner,
                    where
she will keep watch
          until
                    morning.

canticle 72

with pockets full of cash,
    credit cards in hand;
our arms full of $500
       fragrances
and spices used (only)
    by the chefs in the finest
       establishments,
we come,
      to honor you;

but
    you are busy
    going from back door
       to back door
    of every bakery and
      eatery in town,
  gleaning the left-overs
  for your friends at the
      shelter;

you are drenched
    in sweat from head to
         toe,
    hammering nails,
      hanging wallboard,
      installing windows
  at the new house
  for the family
      who spent
  last night sleeping
    in their car;

you are
    at Potters Field,
holding services for
    all the
  Jane and
  John Does
    the world
    has forgotten to
honor.

Epiphany

13

still, waters

like water skimmers,
we simply glide along
the smooth facade of our lives,
   till you come running up,
   diving right in,
   coming up with rivulets
   caressing your big grin,
     as you splash water
     in our eyes so we can
       see;

we drift along
just below the surface,
occasionally coming up for air,
hoping you cannot spy us
hiding in the shadowed pools,
   but you step in
   with your waders on,
   tying the special fly
   the Spirit made for you,
     casting, casting, casting,
     again and again,
       until we take that first bite
       of your grace
       and we are hooked;

throwing caution to the wind,
you drive out onto our frozen souls,
setting up the shack,
chipping through the ice,
dropping your line in the hole,
   patiently waiting   (while you pass the bread
     and bottle around
     with your two buddies)
   to pull us into
     the warmth of your heart.

Baptism of the Lord/Ordinary Time 1

punctuation

i remember those
    (all too many) days
        when the
   ?
  appeared at the end
      of this verse,
   my worries and fears
      always
    trying to boldface it;
there was that one
  time though, when the
       !
   ran up and sang out,
  clear as a bell, that
    shivery afternoon,
   with the wind at my back,
     standing atop
       Dun I;
yet,
    it is there
      on still-as-snow,
       as well as shattering, days;
      in my wondering,
       and wandering, journey;
      in the shadow of my best self,
       and trying to trip up my worst;
    however prosaic,
   seemingly forgettable,
     so grammary,
        but just what i need

'i come to the end—

   i am still with you'

Second Sunday after the Epiphany/Ordinary Time 2

pushy, aren't you?

when,
by the shores of complacency,
i am content to simply
mend the nets
of my washed-up life,
    pull me to my feet,
    plop me in the boat,
    stick the oars in my hand,
    and push me away
        to find the ones
        you would have me
        bring to you;

there,
as i scrape my toes in the dirt
at the city limits
of petulant procrastination,
waiting for the bus to pull up,
    grab the ticket
    to Tarshish out of my hand,
    put on the backpack filled
    with hope and humility,
        and push me towards
        those who have waited
        so long and patiently
            for that simple word
            which can change them
            forever.

Third Sunday after the Epiphany/Ordinary Time 3

the exorcist

what
    are you holding
    in your hands
       (behind your back)
    as you come towards us;

have
    you come to plunge
    the listlessness
    of our lives into
       the pools of your peace,
          or will

 you
    silence the dubious choirs
    which echo 24/7
       in our souls,

 to
    be able to
    expunge those little
    hellions
       who bounce up & down
       on the bedsprings
       of our souls?

do
    for us what you will,
       Holy One of Conundrums,
          for

with
    hope slipping out
    of that tiny tear
    in our heart's pocket,
       and questions piling up
       on the dining room table,
         we wonder,
       if it was left to

 us,
    would we
    embrace your healing touch
       or renounce you
       as the enemy

Jesus of Nazareth?

Fourth Sunday after the Epiphany/Ordinary Time 4

in God's image

when we would gossip
over the pew backs,
whispering behind our hearts,
    you thump our ears,
    silencing our pettiness
    with that 'look' of yours;

when we would
sit in judgment on others,
you dump us
out of our chairs,
taking us by the hand,
    so we can walk with you
    through the alleys,
    past the doorways,
    under the bridges
        to where your children huddle;

when we would stop
to fill up ourselves
with arrogance's free air,
    you puncture our pride
    with the sharp point
    of the gospel,
tsk-tsking,
        'haven't you been
            listening?
    haven't you figured me out
        by now?

you are a servant,

    follow me.'

Fifth Sunday after the Epiphany/Ordinary Time 5

when the time is right

speak . . .

. . .aloud
    for those whose voices
    have been stilled
    by all who know best;
. . .in whispers,
    to a child
    tossing and turning
      in fear's fever;
. . .caroling
    the joy of bathing
    in grace's sweet arms.

keep quiet . . .

. . .tongue-tied
    when caressed
    in a seaside sunset;
. . .tight-lipped
    rather than flapping
    one's gums
      in gossip;
. . .muting
    that inalienable right
    to lash out
      in anger.

there is a time to speak
    as well as a time to be silent . . .

may i discern
the right time,
    Word of my heart.

Sixth Sunday after the Epiphany/Ordinary Time 6

anger

there's that anger
which seems so silly -
afterwards:
>yelling at the person
>ahead of me in traffic;
>wanting to throw my computer
>out the window;
>turning my back on my spouse
>in the middle of an argument.

there's that anger
which seems so satisfying,
so self-righteous:
>i recycle faithfully,
>but my neighbors don't;
>i walk as much as possible,
>while my best friend buys a new SUV;
>knowing i did the job the 'right way'
>while my colleagues all cut corners.

but then,
there's that anger
which doesn't seem to touch me:
>the plight of the homeless
>i see every day on the way to work;
>the encouragement
>not to rock the boat
>by pointing out that most of us
>have more clothes, more shoes, more food
>than we will ever need
>while others have hardly any of anything.

so, like Jesus,
fill me with that anger
that is just, and holy, and you -
>so i can let go of the anger
>that is silly, profane, and only me.

Seventh Sunday after the Epiphany/Ordinary Time 7

canticle 103

you slowly tap the end
            of the pen
        against your lower lip,
                then begin
            writing down all the
            particulars of our lives:
                    poor choices,
                    damaging words spoken aloud,
                    hoarded love,
                    compassion denied;

when you are finished,
        you proof-read
        it three times
            making sure that
                    every peccadillo is punctuated,
                    every i in every sin is dotted,
                    every t in temptation is crossed . . .

. . . staring at us across
                your desk,
        you slowly put
                the thick document
                into the shredder,

and fling the confetti
            into that deepest corner
            of the universe
        where new stars are being born;

and gathering us
upon your lap,
            you simply say,
        'let's try this again.'

Eighth Sunday after the Epiphany/Ordinary Time 8

canticle 81

if
only they **were**
        strange,
    these gods i carry
        so carefully around
        with me –
                success
                narcissism
                bitterness –

but
    they are as
            comfortable
        as the worn slippers
        i put on each
                morning;

if
only they **were**
        foreign (*adj.* from another
                experience),
    these gods i pal
        around with –
                    lust,
                    greed,
            technology –

but
    they are closer
        to me than
        my own siblings
    their seductions
                thicker
        than blood;

if only

Ninth Sunday after the Epiphany/Ordinary Time 9

until

until
we see the faces
of those tossed onto
the world's garbage dumps,
   dazzling bright with
   hope and wholeness;

until
we respect the prophets
we have been yearning for,
   in the hip-hopped, doo-ragged
   teenagers strutting
   through the malls;

until
we hear God's sweet
songs of peace and reconciliation
   in the mother tongues
   of all we turn
   a deaf ear to;

until
we catch a glimpse
of you (out of the corner
of our shut-tight eyes)
   coming down off
   the shelf where we store you
to enter our frayed lives;

maybe
we should have nothing to say . . .

   until

Transfiguration of the Lord

ashes, ashes

burning your covenant
behind me,
i race on ahead
to jump on this
weary-go-round
called life,

sin spinning me
faster and faster,
until i fall off,
dizzily dancing with
death;

getting ready for bed,
i bank the embers
of my ever-faithful fears,
hoping they might
smolder into cold cinders
i can scatter
to the Spirit;

in the morning, i hurriedly
splash my face
with a few handfuls
of the left-over ashes
from yesterday's
feast on foolishness;

ashes, ashes,
we all fall down . . .

into the embrace
of your grace.

Ash Wednesday

like a kitten

my temptations do not come
like a prowling lion
seeking to devour me;
no:
like a kitten,
they curl up in my lap
purring me to complacency.

my desert experience
is not somewhere
'out there' -
it is shuffling papers
at my desk;
dumping another load
of dirty jeans
into the machine;
commuting in my car,
listening to my angry voice
at the drivers around me
echo the ones on the radio.

the Evil One
is too smart to come to me
in a halloween costume
but comes
in the neighbor
a couple of doors down
who fears the way life is changing;
in the knot of teenagers
walking down the street towards me;
in any person, in every person,
who is not my child, my spouse, me.

Tempted One:
strengthen me with your word,
feed me with the sweetness of your grace,
shelter me in the coolness of your love;
then, together,
we can journey to Jerusalem.

First Sunday of Lent

names

traducer
  seducer
    accuser
      persecutor:
all those people i can be
when i follow
  the wrong profit;

rebuker
  quibbler
    nitpicker
      hairsplitter:
of all the faults
i spot so easily
  in those around me;

croaker
  complainer
    grumbler
      mumbler:
every time my life doesn't go
exactly as i asked God
  to create it;

bellyacher
  whiner
    murmurer
      moaner:
when everyone acts
as if it isn't all about
  me;

i've met the enemy
and he is behind me,
  pushing me
  further and further

    from you.

Second Sunday of Lent

decalogue

we kept scuffing out
those ten words with
our shifty lives:

    crossing the boundary
      of a vowed relationship;

    taking the breath away
      from one of your
        children;

    leaning over the backyard
      fence
    to sow weeds
      in a friend's
        heart;

so we would not
keep thinking we
were so wise,

    you took
    a piece of wood
        and
    drew a line
      in our souls

which death,
    disappointment,
      chaos
can never erase.

Third Sunday of Lent

snakebit

slowly,
so leisurely
i do not take notice,
   the dullness of sin
   wraps itself about
      my fluttering hopes
(until i can no longer
   see my soul
         in front of me);

slyly,
      whispering comforting
      words of emptiness,
   my murmurs of discontent
   meander through my heart
until they become
the only voice
        i trust;

sinuously,
      with a wink,
         a turn of the head,
   a flicker of its tongue,
success wends its way
around my faith
      squeezing tighter and tighter
until i have no breath
      left
   to offer praises.

but with the sharp point
      of a nail,
you excise my wounds,
anointing them with grace,
   wrapping them in
   the balm of your
      love.

Fourth Sunday of Lent

28

wishing

i wish to see Jesus:
in the panhandler on Main Street –
but the unkempt hair,
the stained, tattered clothes,
the odors fit for a barnyard
cloud my eyes;

i wish to hear Jesus:
in the politicians
making decisions i cannot support;
in the evangelist
mouthing platitudes to the pain-full;
in the talk-show callers
spewing hateful bile;
but their words
clog my ears;

i wish to meet Jesus:
in the tattooed skateboarder
riding the rails at the school;
in the hip-hopper
jamming at the bus stop;
in the goths hanging outside
the video arcade,
but too quickly i cross the street
looking for him in folks
just like me.

Jesus:
why would you wish

to see
to hear
to meet
me?

Fifth Sunday of Lent

palmassion

joy dances down
the street,
grabbing us by the hand,
twirling us round
and round
as glad tears and songs
make a carpet
of welcome
for the one who comes.
but later . . .

we'll strip the branches
to weave
a cross;
stones that echoed
        'hosanna!'
will bloody the knees
of the stumbling
servant;

we'll dust off
our cloaks
and swaddle ourselves
to ward off
the cold breath
of death
sweeping down
from the Skull.

and when we
look back at everything
we could have
done
        it will be
        too late.

Palm/Passion Sunday

Mary took a pound of costly perfume made of pure nard, anointed Jesus' feet, and wiped them with her hair. The house was filled with the fragrance of the perfume. (John 12:3)

because

we have preserved our grace
in manna jars
for the long winter of despair,
storing them in the dark corners
of our souls,
we have forgotten
its gritty taste;

because
we have put a tight lid
on our joy,
and put it in the back
of the pantry,
we have forgotten
how it can tickle
our noses;

because
we are so busy
prattling pious platitudes
about the poor, the least, the lost,
we ignore your words
which anoint them
as your children;

because
we have put up
the shutters and storm doors
to keep your future
from sneaking in,
we have missed
the sweet breeze
carrying your hope
to us;

because
we are who we are,
restore us, Holy Grace,
and make us
a fragrant offering to the world.

Holy Monday

31

Now among those who went up to worship at the festival were some Greeks.
They came to Philip, who was from Bethsaida in Galilee, and said to him,
"Sir, we wish to see Jesus." (John 12:20-21)

our eyes

our eyes
easily slide past the
disheveled, hollow-eyed
fellow with the
hand printed sign:
'wounded vet cannot find work
have mercy on me';

our eyes
constantly
flickering to
our car's touchscreen,
we do not
notice the old woman
bundled in three
coats on a
summer's day,
pushing her cart
with her life piled
high in it;

our eyes
glued to our
handheld device
while dragging
our dog on the
early morning
walk, we miss
the kids on the
corner
selling baked goods
for a classmate's
chemo costs;

we could see you,
Jesus,
but we are
usually looking
the other way.

Holy Tuesday

After saying this Jesus was troubled in spirit, and declared, "Very truly, I tell you, one of you will betray me.". . . When he had gone out, Jesus said, "Now the Son of Man has been glorified, and God has been glorified in him. If God has been glorified in him, God will also glorify him in himself and will glorify him at once." (John 13:21, 31-32)

kitchen whispers

taking the tray
from the server,
she slides the dirty
dishes
into the warm, soapy
water;

turning,
she grabs the pots
and pans,
banging them as
loudly
as she can, muttering
(not so softly)
to herself, "there he
goes again,
talking in riddles
that no one can
solve. why
can't he just come
out and say
things plainly?"

turning from
the door where
she is eavesdropping,
Mary hushes, 'quiet,
sister! I think
this may be
important.'

Holy Wednesday

33

Jesus, knowing that the Father had given all things into his hands, and that he had come from God and was going to God, got up from the table, took off his outer robe, and tied a towel around himself. Then he poured water into a basin and began to wash the disciples' feet and to wipe them with the towel that was tied around him. He came to Simon Peter, who said to him, "Lord, are you going to wash my feet?" Jesus answered, "You do not know now what I am doing, but later you will understand." (John 13:3-7)

uncomfortable . . .

. . . that's how we
feel, when
the basin of
water is
set before us,
the gentle ripples
of your love
caressing the
surface of that
life
of service
to which you
call us,

yet
we cannot bring
ourselves
to even dip
just our toes
in;

and it won't
be
until tomorrow
that we realize
what you are
really doing
is
showing us
you
will never,
ever,
wash your hands
of
us.

Holy Thursday

excarnation

a mother
once again cradles
her son, swaddling
him in
soft garments woven
from her grief;

shepherds stand gazing
from a nearby
hillside,
weeping at all
they had seen and
heard;

myrrh is taken from
the back shelf
where it has
gathered dust
through all the
years;

and angels
weep
silently
as
Jesus
returns home
by
another
road.

Holy Friday

the dust man

pushing his wheeled
bin before him,
the trash collector
goes on his early
morning rounds

throwing a handful
of bent, bloodied,
nails
onto the piles of
dreams turned
to ashes;

bundling up
the splintered
crossbeam
cast aside after
the latest
execution;

gathering
the empty wine
bottles, the cup and die
the soldiers left
behind before
heading off
to guard duty
at the graveyard;

and tossing a
cracked board
which read "King
of the Jews"
in three languages
on top of all
the other
fragments of
faith,

he trundles down
the hill into
misty
silence.

Holy Saturday

early

early in the morning
you put the brightly
colored eggs and
chocolate goodies
in all the baskets piled
high with plastic grass,
giving them to E. B.
to deliver while you
went back to bed . . .

(no?)

early in the morning
you put on your
invisibility cloak and
after stupefying
the guards, you
waved your wand,
rolling the stone
away . . .

(no?)

early in the morning
Jesus felt around
the floor of the
tomb,
until he found
the bag in the corner,
and pulling on the
tights, as well as the shirt
with the big red S,
he broke the stone
into a million pieces,
and flew off, his cape
flapping in the wind . . .

(still no?
okay then, how about)

very
early in the morning
when our fears were
still in their cups,
you sat in the darkness,
cradling your silenced
Word,
as your tears
carved rivers through
chaos, and your
voice cracked with anguish
as you whispered,

'let there be life'

and

he is   .

Easter

springtime of doubts

as my frozen heart
thaws bit by bit,
   and the brown lawn
   carpeting my soul
   begins to green,
      they appear:

slowly
tenaciously
   they push up
   through the tangled
   roots of my belief

their bright heads
dazzling in the light,
   the softness of
   their caresses
   inviting me to pause
     (just for a moment),
   to lie down and
   contemplate their beauty,
     to stay in their midst
     a little while longer;

then
you come along,
gathering them up
into your arms,
   appearing a little
   while later,
a luscious salad
tossed from their leaves,
     the petals pressed
     into a chardonnay
  (with a hint of
    of peace),
all placed on the Table

a part of the feast
you have prepared
   for us.

Second Sunday of Easter

show and tell

if we showed you
our hands,
would you find them nicked
from building a house
for the homeless;
or a callous on our thumb
from using the TV remote
too much?

if we showed you
our feet,
would you find them toughened
by walking the corridors
of a hospice
with the terminally ill;
or wrinkled
by too many hours
in the hot tub?

if we showed you
our hearts,
would you find them broken
over the struggles of
the lost, the little, the last, the least;
or would they be clogged
with the plaque
of our consumerized lives?

if we truly want to be
your witnesses,
God of the empty grave,
would you show us
how?

Third Sunday of Easter

canticle 23

with you at my side,
i am not poverty-stricken:
    finding rest in your lush love,
    stilling myself by baptismal pools,
        dipping my frantic feet
        in the cool waters;
    you add zest
    to my fading impishness,
        you carve your name
        in each paving stone
            set in the path.

when fear, sickness, doubt
crook their finger at me
from the shadows,
    i can lean on
    your walking stick
    to make my way to
that table where
my rivals are seated;

you pour healing oil out
for dipping the bread of life,
    the cup of grace spills over
    staining my hands with hope.

Shirley, Goodness, Mercy
(my childhood friends)
and i play follow the leader
    till we end up
    on the front porch,
you welcoming us with
wide-open arms of joy.

Fourth Sunday of Easter

41

. . . may i . . .

in the secret places,
where fears and doubts
litter the floor of my heart,
you come along
    sweeping them into your dustpan,
    exposing the bright foundation of faith;

you sit me on your lap,
placing your hand over mine,
stretching out my finger,
    so, together, we trace
    the words in the stories
    of grace and hope
    told (and lived out)
        in each generation;

you could roam all the ends of creation,
but choose to hang out
with me (!)
    grabbing me by the hand
    when i am about to dart out
    into the traffic on Sin Street;
        lifting me into the air
        to reach the highest branch
        so i can swing
            back-and-forth
            on the Arm of your love.

        Mother . . .
        . . .may i always
        lose my heart to
            you.

Fifth Sunday of Easter

42

old songs

we love the old songs:

we hum to ourselves
the old, old story
and feel like we are slipping on
a frayed, comfortable shirt
which will keep us warm;

we sing in the shower
of all those places
where the saints have trod,
and wonder what ever
happened to them;

the fears of aging
jerk us awake
in the middle of the night
and into the silence
of our souls
we whisper
'Jesus loves me, this i know,
for the Bible tells me so . . .'

we love the old songs so much
we might miss the new ones:

the sunrise announcing
a new beginning each day;

the laughter of children,
louder than despair's dirge;

the softness
of a parent's love
which smoothes our rough edges;

teach us new songs,
Joyous Heart,
teach us new songs.

Sixth Sunday of Easter

while

we may think
      witnessing
    is going from house to house
      hanging flyers on
      the doorknob

but it is
      while
    we help a refugee
    sound out the words
      in her new language;
    mentor a student in
    the complexities of
      simple algebra;
    send a box of books
    to that school whose
      library flooded,
that the gospel is
      preached.

we may see robes, stoles,
    hoods and preaching tabs
    as signs of power

but it is
      while
    we wear an apron
      in the soup kitchen,
    or a tool belt
      at the house-building site,
    or a gown and a mask
      as we enter a hospital room,
that we are clothed
      as your servants.

it is
      while
    you are blessing us
      that
    we are sent to bless
      others.

Ascension

canticle 1

we walk on air,
when we refuse to go to
the self-help seminar
    hosted by Incorrigibles, Inc.;

when we won't put our feet
in the footprints left
by those who trespass
    through life;
when we refuse
to sit down in the seats
    vacated by the skeptics;

        rather,
God tickles us pink
by handing us that credo
    which we can chew on,
    in silence and hope,
        until we hunger for nothing else.
rooted deeply in grace and mercy,
    we yield a harvest
    in every season of life,
        our gifts do not need
        to be raked up and taken
            to the landfill -
    we turn out well.

the reprobates are polar opposites:
    blown about like dandelion
        puffs;
they won't be able
    to break in line ahead of us,
    or sit in the front row;

God sweeps the litter
    the vandals have thrown
    on the sidewalk,
and watches us play
    hopscotch all day long.

Seventh Sunday of Easter

45

come

when the Spirit comes,
   she will put dancing shoes
   on my two left feet,
     lace them up
     and lead me out
     onto the floor,
   where we will enter
   the Argentine Tango
     competition;

when the Spirit comes,
   she will wander through
   the barren garden of my soul,
   and
     as she opens her hands,
     butterflies will skitter
     from withered hope
       to dashed dream,
   breathing them back
        to life;

when the Spirit comes,
   and finds me brooding
   by the stagnant pool of tears,
     she will dive right in,
     drenching me with God's joy,
       then teach me how
       to float on my back
        (without sinking)
   pointing out the flames
   flitting about our heads
     like fireflies.

come,
     Spirit,
come . . .

Day of Pentecost

46

the juggler

i toss
    God
  into the air,
    watching the divine
  spin and sparkle
      in the   air;
next i add
    Jesus
  to the mix, carefully
    throwing each
     from one hand
       to the
     other, confident
  i will not drop either
      One;
then, pulling
    Spirit
  from my back pocket, i begin
  that simply
      complex
  process of keeping all
    Three
      in the air;
as i settle
into the rhythm
of keeping the
     holy community
  under my control
  (propelling them
    faster and faster
     until they
    become a
    blur no one can
    comprehend),
  the audience sits
     spellbound
  by my theological
    dexterity,
and none of us
      hear
  your gentle whisper,
  'why do you think
  it is all an
    act?'

Trinity Sunday

47

hineni

lying in the shadows
>of the 3rd hour,
>>i thought i heard your
>>>whimper, but
>when i looked
>>out the window,
>>it was only the neighbor's wife
>>crying again
>>>on her back porch;

head down,
>tracking the words
>on my phone's tiny screen,
>i thought i heard
>>you call my name, but
>>>when i turned
>>>around,
>there was
>>>>nobody
>but a straggly-haired
>>fellow
>with his hopes
>>held out;

on the bus,
>engrossed in the
>sounds from my
>>>buds,
>i felt a tug
>on my sleeve,
>>but it was only
>>a little boy
>holding out his foot
>with the untied shoe;

here i am,
>Lord,

where do you want
me
to serve?

Second Sunday after Pentecost/Ordinary Time 9

out of harm's way

petition in hand
  you are about
      to go
    out the door,
ready to stop
every person
        in the street,
asking them to fight
  against today's
      injustice,

but
    we grab
          you
  right before
    you grasp the
        doorknob
imploring
        "but we haven't
  finished breakfast"

pulling on your
        winter coat,
  and wrapping a muffler
    around your neck,
you pick up the box of
        sandwiches
    for the overnight
        shelter,

  but
      we walk over,
dangling the car keys
    in front of you,
        coldly stating,
  "you're not going anywhere
    with the roads so
        icy."

49

turning Rublev's
         Trinity
towards the
  wall;

forgetting to pick
  up your clothes
  at the cleaners
   (again! really?);
hiding your sandals
     in the back of the
  closet,

we can come up
with dozens of ways to
       restrain
     you
  from bringing the
    kingdom

into
     our lives,

   our churches,

     our world.

Third Sunday after Pentecost/Ordinary Time 10

seeds

it's the
word of confidence
to a 9-year-old
which one day leads to
the winning goal
in a World Cup match;

it's the
extra practice sessions
after school,
going over word after word,
which bolsters
a young girl
at the Spelling Bee Nationals;

it's the gentle touch
of a mother
in the terror of
a midnight thunderstorm
which leads a child
into nursing;

in a world
which idolizes
success, greatness,
biggie-sized achievements,
remind us
of those mustard seeds
planted deep within us
by so many over the years,
which help to shape us
into the people
you mean us to be,
Tender God.

Fourth Sunday after Pentecost/Ordinary Time 11

in the still of the night

i can cross the t's
and dot every i
  in my doctrinal
  blue book
  during the mid-terms,
    but cast off
    into my dusky life
    as the storm clouds
    gather on the horizon?

i can (intellectually)
affirm certain teachings
  (though that predestination
  thingy has always bugged me,
  but you knew that before the
  foundations of the world
  were poured, right?)
    but calmly, without a whimper,
    resist crawling under the covers
    when lightning strikes
    and thunder rumbles
      through my heart?

i can memorize
all the creeds
and parrot every
confession of faith,
  but keep on steering
  through the waves
  crashing over my soul
    without looking over
    my shoulders to see
      if you have woken up?

what do you think
i am

    faithfull?

Fifth Sunday after Pentecost/Ordinary Time 12

canticle 130

i dangle my toes over
   the curb of my heart,
      my toes washed in
those tears racing
   towards the storm drain,
my keening words
      echoing through the
         empty streets;

if you wrote all my sins
on the blackboard
you would run out of schools,
   but the Spirit stays after class,
   banging dusty death out of the
      erasers
begging your pardon
for Crossing
      out your work;

more than those
who watch the clock
on the graveyard shift,
   i wait (we wait!) for hope
   to be the lyrics of
      the music of your heart,
more than a rooster
scanning the horizon
for that first glimpse of dawn -

we hope
   for you . . .

Sixth Sunday after Pentecost/Ordinary Time 13

dust shaker

unmoved
by the cries
of the poor,
　shake the dust
　out of our ears
　　so we can listen;

uncompassionate
to the brokenness
of our own kind,
　shake the dust
　off our hearts
　　so we can give them
　　　away;

callous
towards those
different from us,
　shake the dust
　from our souls
　　so we may embrace them;

amassed
by years of hoarding,
　shake the dust
　off our nest eggs of
　　　blessing,
　　so we may offer grace
　　to the hopeless;

shake the dust
off our unbelief,
Son of Mary,
　so the gospel
　might be lived in
　　　us.

Seventh Sunday after Pentecost/Ordinary Time 14

musically challenged

i would prefer
to be left
leaning against the wall,
shuffling my two left feet,
watching the world
twirl by;
but you take me by the hand
to teach me
the dance steps
of grace;

when i walk near
the piano,
it shudders,
hoping
i will not sit down;
but you take my fingers
and place them on the keys,
whispering,
"play, play with joy, play!"

even with
the biggest bucket,
i can't carry a tune;
but you push me
out onto the stage,
introducing me as
the new soloist
in the Good News Choir.

i will celebrate your joy,
sing your hope,
play your love,
leaping and whirling
in your grace
forever!

Eighth Sunday after Pentecost/Ordinary Time 15

building

me -
   a dwelling place for God?

my roof
     leaks with wayward
     and wanton thoughts . . .

my windows
     look out on a world
     lusting for more
        and caring for less;
     if any dare peek in,
        they will see the same hungers . . .

my furnace
     is filled with the ashes
        of dusty dreams
        and hapless hopes . . .

my foundation
   cracks under the weight of loneliness,
   ravaged by the storms of sadness.

i would build you
     a house, my God:

           re-build me
           instead.

Ninth Sunday after Pentecost/Ordinary Time 16

only

we sit down
with our sharpened pencils,
to chart out the
longitude and latitude
of your grace
    only
        to keep running
        out of paper;

we tie a string
around each sin,
dropping them into
your sea of forgiveness,
    only
        to discover we can
        never plumb its depths;

we scrabble and scrape,
push and pummel ourselves
from Land's End to John o' Groats
on our self-planned journey,
    only
        to find
        we are at the
        starting point
        of your Way;

how foolish we are
to try to limit you
by our imagination
    only.

Tenth Sunday after Pentecost/Ordinary Time 17

prayer

some day,
i would like to learn
how to pray:

oh,
i can hammer words together
to make a nice box
for you to fill
with what i am sure i need:
    but i falter
    when i try to climb out
    of that hole of hopelessness
    i find myself in;

i can bring you
my scrapbook filled
with all the stories
of the brokenness of the world:
    but the pages
    of my dreams, my fears,
    my fickle faith
    are out in the trashcan;

i can race to you
to tattle on
all my friends and neighbors
so you will know where all the mud-stains
on their lives come from:
    but in my haste
    to get to you first,
    i stumble over
    the shadowed secrets
    in my soul.

some day,
i would like to learn how to pray,
Listening God.

Eleventh Sunday after Pentecost/Ordinary Time 18

habits

anger is the ulcer
in our souls
that causes sleepless nights;

lies are the stones
we pile
on top of each other
until we have built
a wall
between us and another;

our words
   muttered in malice
   or
   hurled like lightning
are the weapons of mass destruction
   in the deserts of our lives.

all the habits
of our hearts
   that break yours,
   Gentle One,
we would let go of
so we might be held
in your grace.

Twelfth Sunday after Pentecost/Ordinary Time 19

doxology

you tiptoe into our rooms
while the shadows still dream,
gently touching our hearts until
we roll over and open our eyes;
    putting a finger to your lips,
    you whisper, 'get up, sleepyheads,
    i want you to see something.'

with our hands wrapped
around steaming cups, we sit
sidebyside on the lawn, comfortable
  as only
    soul friends can be,

watching the kitten stalk a butterfly
through the wildflower jungle,
softly laughing as the monarch
glides gracefully,
    (so tantalizingly) just out of reach.

breaking off a piece of toast,
you pop it into our mouths,
and as it slowly incarnates
deep, so deep, within us,
  we lean our heads
  on your shoulder,
  with a drowsy,
    'thanks for everything.'

Thirteenth Sunday after Pentecost/Ordinary Time 20

the answer

No!
I cannot follow you
right now:
your words are too hard,
your road is too long,
your life is too demanding,
your death is too frightening.

Maybe . . .
i could follow you:
in a few days
when the weekend comes
(but those are 'days off,' you understand);
in a few months
after school has begun
and the Thanksgiving crowd is gone
(but then come the hectic days of Christmas
and all that means - surely you understand);
in a few years
after i've done what i want,
after the kids are gone,
after the work is done
(i'm sure you understand).

YES!
i will follow you:
trusting my heart,
trusting your words,
trusting you, Lord.

which answer
will i give today,
my God?

Fourteenth Sunday after Pentecost/Ordinary Time 21

through us

if we would be your people,
Blessed God,
we must look in the windows of the world:
    to see as you see,
    to love as you love,
    to act as you act.

through us,
you would
    stand by the poor,
    rescuing them
    at the beginning of their distress,
    not when they are
    at the end of their hope.

through us,
you would
    side with the oppressed,
    and challenge us
    to release them
    from their tyranny and torture.

through us,
you would
    speak for the voiceless,
    and call the powerful
    to meek and lowly lives.

through us,
you would . . .

Beloved Holy One:
    help us to be doers,
        not just hearers
    of your heart.

Fifteenth Sunday after Pentecost/Ordinary Time 22

ephphatha

if we turn up our radios
or CD players loud enough,
O God,
we are able to deafen the cries
of the needy and oppressed:

be opened, ears!

if we switch channels quickly,
O God,
we do not have to see those disturbing images
of the children in the barrios of Brazil
or the families in Gaza:

be opened, eyes!

if we are persistent enough in our pharisaism,
and diligent enough with our doctrines,
O God,
we can keep 'them' from coming to the Table,
keeping it all (even the crumbs) for ourselves:

be opened, arms!

if we are cool towards the passions
of pesky outsiders,
if we are indifferent to the injustices
of our world,
O God,
we can remain apathetic
in the face of grace being poured out
for our parched spirits:

be opened, hearts!

Sixteenth Sunday after Pentecost/Ordinary Time 23

say what?

at the end,
just before the bell
rings,
i bring my blue books
(filled with
observations from my favorite
theologs;
answers [copied almost word-for-word]
from the 2 volumes
Calvin wrote;

quotations from all the
parables
you gave over the length
of the course [just to prove
i was paying attention,
though my eyes appeared
closed];

minutes from all the judicatory
meetings and committees
i attended;

copies of all the sermons
where i managed to turn the
good news
into gobbledygook)
up to your desk,
where you set them on top
of all the others,
and taking a match
you set them all on fire,

as
you tap me on the
chest, asking,
'what's in here?'

Seventeenth Sunday after Pentecost/Ordinary Time 24

tumbling act

not by marching round and round
seven times (or more),
but by simply
standing still;

not in great tumult
or loud curses,
but by a gracious,
welcoming invitation;

not with a parable
or recounting of past
wonders and might,
but by a gentle
affirmation:

the meek find their voice,
blind trust becomes the path to walk,
futures are put at risk,
masks are taken off,
walls fall down

in jericho.

Eighteenth Sunday after Pentecost/Ordinary Time 25

the numbered ones
        come in handy,
    when we are trying
        to decide
        who's in/who's out,
    who should we reach
        out to, using all
        sorts of demographics
            and stats, deciding
        whether or not the budget
    can fund that proposed
        ministry;
we've taken them
            out
        to spell
I-M-M-I-G-R-A-N-T
    to make sure others
            know their
            place,
    or
D-0-C-T-R-I-N-E
            so no one
        can do well
    on the entrance exam,
        or
            C-L-O-S-E-D
    so our afternoon
    committee meetings
    won't be interrupted
        by folks searching
        for a friend
            (or you);
but you
reach into the
            toy box
        grabbing up all
    the blocks in your
            arms
and begin
        to build your
        kingdom
            which
    is for
everyone.

finding

we will not find
the justice we need
        with our apathy;
we will not find
the unity which eludes us
        with our quarreling;
we will not find
the wholeness we yearn for
        with our doctrines;
we will not find
the love we have misplaced
        with our hating;
we will not find
the rest we crave
        with our exhausting schedules;
we will not find
the peace we seek
        with our silence;

but

we will find you
        in the brokenness of the Bread
        and the cracking of our hearts;

we will find you
        when we empty the Cup,
        refill it with our gifts
        and offer it to a little child;

we will find you
        when we make room at the Table
        for all your people.

Twentieth Sunday after Pentecost/Ordinary Time 27

at the fragile edges

what can i do
to get that Christmas present:
- play nice with my kid sister;
- put away my toys at night;
- eat (all!?!) my vegetables?

what should i do
to deserve a brighter day:
- whistle rather than whine;
- smile at that person i'd like to smack;
- put a dollar (nothing smaller in my pocket,
darn it!) in the handler of the pan?

what must i do
to earn eternal life:
- not let my eyes wander over another;
- cough that gossip germ into my elbow;
- drop enough sins so i can squeeze through the gate?

at the fragile edges
of life,
where you lived and spoke
with the poor,
the possessed,
the children,
the outcasts:
was that where you discovered
even **you** could not save
yourself

and,
let go of all that you were,
so that with God
every thing became
possible
for us?

Twenty-first Sunday after Pentecost/Ordinary Time 28

able

hand me a
steaming cuppa,
swirling with just
the right mixture of milk and sugar,
and i am content
to curl up in my chair,
listening to you
all day;

but offer me
your chipped, stained mug
filled with that vinegary
mix of discipleship and obedience,
well,
you'll forgive me (i'm sure)
if it slips through my fingers,
shattering on the cold, hard
floor of my soul.

i'd belly flop eagerly
(and all too easily)
into those warm
baptismal waters,
floating the rest of my life,
stretched out on my back,
watching the clouds
drift by, over my head;

but your invitation
to skinny dip in your
drudgery filled pool,
dodging death's icebergs
as they drift by?
you'll understand (i hope)
if i let someone else
go in ahead of me.
disabled by my penchant
for power and privilege,

how can i ever
do whatever
you
ask of me?

Twenty-second Sunday after the Pentecost/Ordinary Time 29

sitting duck

i would wear
steel-toed boots
to nudge my friends
out of the way,
or high-heeled wellies
so i am not dirtied
by the muck of the world,
  but you rub
  my Achilles' heel raw
  with the pebble of
  servanthood;

i would take
self-defense courses
to protect myself
from all the blows
the world throws at me,
  but you pull off
  my gloves
  and show me
  the wide open stance
  of grace;

i would build a fence
of cynicism and doubt
around my soul
so no one can sneak past
with their pain and need,
  but you hold out
  your heart to me,
  naked and bleeding
  from its brokenness.

Jesus, Son of David,
have pity on me:
so when I want to be
safe and secure,
i can become a sitting duck
for your vulnerability.

Twenty-third Sunday after the Pentecost/Ordinary Time 30

roadmap

sitting on a park bench,
trying to center yourself
     in silence and prayer,
  a little boy sits down
  with a book in his hand
  asking you to read a
     difficult passage;
finished, you ask, 'do you
     understand what it means?'
  and he smiles and whispers,
     'not far.'

grabbing the heavy bags
  out of the car, you
  carry the groceries
  in for your neighbor,
 helping her to put them
    away;
finished, she pours two
     glasses
  of cold water,
  and touching hers
     to yours,
 toasts, 'not far.'

pulling your car onto
     the shoulder,
  on a wintery, bitter day,
 you help a single mom
  with three little ones
    in the back seat
  change a flat tire;
finished, she gets back
  in the car, and
  rolling down the window
     points off in the
   distance,
'not far.'

Twenty-fourth Sunday after Pentecost/Ordinary Time 31

saint lucy

st. lucy stopped for a moment
while she rested her arms and legs
from pushing her little
brother down the sidewalk
in his electric car whose
battery had run down;
stroking Maya's nose,
her eyes shimmered with delight
and she exploded in a giggle,
'you're a silly dog!'
when she suddenly baptized her
with a sloppy kiss.

pausing for a few moments
from helping his elderly neighbor,
st. chuck leaned on his rake,
smiling as his grandkids,
eagerly and deliberately
scattered the leaves he had
spent all afternoon carefully
piling by the curb,
whispering, 'what a life!'

slowly, painstakingly, as if
she were joining together a puzzle,
differently-abled st. jennifer
put each item in its place
in the cloth bags,
not making them too heavy
(as the customer requested)
making sure the bread
ended up on top,
and nothing too heavy
was near the eggs.

they're all around us, aren't they,
those precious drops of grace
sprinkled in our lives?

All Saints' Day

canticle 127

unless you keep giving us
the kingdom's vocabulary test,
until we know your hopes
backwards and forwards,
we hem-and-haw
on the part of the have-nots,
our words wobbling weekly
past the world's ears;

unless you take your fingers
and rub the avarice
out of our eyes,
we drift further and further
away from our sisters and brothers,
leaving them buffeted and bruised
on poverty's floor;

unless you fashion our hearts
into a sanctuary
for your compassion,
we can only hand out
the moldy bread
of futility,
we can only offer a drink
from the cup filled
with empty promises.

unless you . . .

Twenty-fifth Sunday after Pentecost/Ordinary Time 32

shiloh

you wait
    at shiloh,

where we can bring
   our brokenness
      and,
  with the pebbles
    formed from our tears,
  the rocks chiseled
    from our hardened
         hearts,
  the stones others
    have cast at us,
      we build a
   cairn
to mark this place
  as holy ground;

   at shiloh,

where our cries
    are
       plainted
  with the mother
  who cannot afford
    medicine for her
      child,
  with the teenager
  whose heart bleeds
     first love,
  with the family
  whose future has been
      foreclosed,
  we whisper
    our aching loneliness
  to the listening
      One;

at shiloh,

where our worst
is enveloped by your
best,
where our emptiness
is filled
at your table of
grace,

where our despair
is transformed by your
hope;

at shiloh,

you wait . . .

Twenty-sixth Sunday after Pentecost/Ordinary Time 33

truth

what is truth?

kings are old,
or dead:
dust collecting on
history's bookshelf;

so,
why would we need
kings
(or 'constitutional monarchs')
in this day of ipods/mp3s,
lightning fast email,
instant connect with anyone,
anywhere,
anytime
in the world?

what is truth?

truth is a commodity
traded to the highest bidder;
truth is a documentary
based on a novel;
truth is what comes out
of the end of a gun;

what is truth?

Truth is who you are,
Jesus
(who would be enthroned
in my heart, if I only would
let you),
as we discover
chasing to catch up with you:
and Truth is what you do,
on the cross,
dying for Pilate,
for Israel,
for feckless disciples,

for me.

Reign of Christ/Christ the King

no easy thanks

it will be easy
to be filled with gratitude
for friends and family
as we gather together:
    so make us mindful
    of the lonely,
    the friendless,
    the forgotten.

it will be easy
to lift a prayer of thanks
as i carve the turkey
this week:
    so give me the words
    to speak out
    for the mother in Darfur
    cradling her hungry child
    in her arms.

it will be easy
to be filled with hope
as we take a long walk
after such a big meal,
and enjoy the freedom to do so:
    so help us to remember
    those held captive
    by violence and war,
    by addiction and pain,
    by brokenness and despair.

it would be easy
to simply give thanks:
    so intensify my compassion,
    broaden my concern,
    enlarge my heart
  with your grace.

Thanksgiving Day

post-election prayer

the TV ads are history:
now
let us see one another
as sisters and brothers;

the vitriolic words have faded:
now
let us speak
of community,
of integrity,
of shared commitment;

the fists that were shaken
at opponents are unclenched:
now
let them reach out
to lift up the fallen,
to open a book for a child,
to serve a meal to the hungry,
to offer a job to the one
standing by the side
of society.

Election Day is over,
Healing God,
now
let us live together,
laugh together,
envision together,
serve together.

Amen.

ABOUT THE AUTHOR

Thom M. Shuman is a graduate of Eckerd College (St. Petersburg, FL) and Union Presbyterian Seminary (Richmond, VA). Currently active in transitional/interim ministry, he has served churches in Oklahoma, Virginia, and Ohio. His liturgies, poems, and prayers are used by congregations all over the world, and by individuals for personal devotions.

His Advent devotional books *The Jesse Tree* (2005) and *Gobsmacked* (2011) have been published by Wild Goose Publications/The Iona Community (www.ionabooks.com), as well as his wedding liturgy, *Now Come Two Hearts*. *Lenten and Easter Nudges* (PDF download) was published in 2013, as was *Advent Nudges* (PDF download) by Wild Goose Publications. He is a contributor to the Iona Community's Resource books *Candles & Conifers, Hay & Stardust, Fire and Bread, Bare Feet and Buttercups,* and *Acorns and Archangels*, as well as *Going Home Another Way: Daily Readings and Resources for Christmastide, Gathered and Scattered: Readings and Meditations from the Iona Community, 50 New Prayers From The Iona Community,* and *Like Leaves to the Sun, Prayers from the Iona Community.*

Where the Broken Gather, a book of liturgies with communion for Lectionary Year B, is a companion to *Dust Shaker.*

Dusty the Church Dog and other sightings of the gospel has recently been published.

Bearers of Grace and Justice, a book of liturgies with communion for Lectionary Year C was published in 2012, as well as its companion book, *Pirate Jesus, poems and prayers for Lectionary Year C. Playing Hopscotch in Heaven, Lectionary Liturgies for RCL Year A* was published in 2013, as well as its companion, *Piano Man.*

He blogs at www.occasionalsightings.blogspot.com
www.prayersfortoday.blogspot.com
www.lectionaryliturgies.blogspot.com

Extracts from the New Revised Standard Bible © Copyright © 1989, by the Division of Christian Education of the National Council of the Churches of Christ in the United States of America. Used by permission. All rights reserved.

79

37338847R00050

Made in the USA
Lexington, KY
30 November 2014